When Did It Aall Gan Wrang?

Alan Baker
and other voices

OPEN HOUSE EDITIONS

Published by Open House Editions
An imprint of Leafe Press
www.leafepresspoetry.com

ISBN: 978-1-7397213-0-5

Cover: Detail from Thomas Oliver's map of Newcastle and
Gateshead, 1830.

CONTENTS

Ten Tyneside Twittersonnets

when did it aall gan wrang?

kids need a good sla
pin little tramps ca
nnit leave nowt alae
n - fancy pinchin' m
e flowers eeh mann a
would've bought them
some theor's fly-tip
pin eggin ya hoose i
sn't safe nee pub cl
ub shops nee communi
ty centre nowt for k
ids used ti be a can
ny place when did it
aall gan wrang mrs t

the auld gadgy ti
the young barman (1977)

o yi courtin yet son?
lassies! ye divint w
anna bother with the
m mann, aa niver did
wey no man, aa'm kno
ckin on a bit noo, b
ut aa still like the
laddies. aye, a bonny
lad like ye. aa've n
iver telt anyone bef
ore. o christ! divin
t tell the lads in h
eor will ye? aa divi
n knaa wot thid dee!

written doon

alreet myet! wiy liv
es in that hoos? why
di aa wanna knaa? co
s aa used ti live th
eor mysel, then aa w
ent doon sooth -to s
underland? wey no ma
nn! a cyem back jist
ti talk ti people o
mebbees jis ti taalk
ti mysel, or mebbees
jus ti write doon wa
words - mine n yours
a mean –thit a've ni
va seen written doon

wor Thomas (1937)

sundae mornings he'd
say howay doon the q
uayside wi me wor ki
d six bairns mam & d
ad grandma in two ro
oms we wor hungry bu
t we nivor ailed a t
hing till wor Tom ca
ught a fever nee mon
ey nee doctor. still
just a laddie. me ma
m's hair torned whit
e owaneet neebody be
lieves iz but it did

Charlie Carr speaks (1977)

they can hadaway and
shite the lorra them
they're wor shipyard
s noo, wi sweated to
build them ships pro
od o them an aall wi
are, me faatha his f
aatha worked for now
t and noo we'll get
what wi desorve, the
fruits of wa labours
aa divint blame yi s
on for leavin toon &
gittin' an education

wa leins are open 24/7

aye, aa can dee that
for yi, nee bother m
ann, wey aye, alreet
if yi say so missus,
aa'm heor ti help aa
l day aal neet, aa c
an offa yi a canny p
rice, we'll help yi,
aye, divint fash yas
sel mann, a knaa yiz
are not happy not wo
rking it's knackered
heve yi tried tornin
it off, then on agen

second lad oot

giz a deek o ya comi
c son. See that stor
y aboot the sowjers?
that was me crossing
the Rhine, 1945 nee
kiddin mann. that I
ad theor the forst I
ad oot the baet, he
was killed. aa was t
he second one oot. n
ee maer questions bo
nny lad. it's ower i
t was a lang teim ag
o he winnit come back

it doesn't soond reet

when aa say howay la
ds and lasses, wi ga
nna form a governmen
t, it doesn't soond
reet. when aa say aa
've aalways wanted t
i dae astrophysics,
it doesn't soond reet.
when aa recite poetr
y when aa record me
voicemyel, say no. 8
even when aa say it
doesn't soond reet,
it doesn't soond reet.

canny sayings

wi's ganna be the on
e ti hoy the forst s
tane? hev yi niva do
ne oot wrang yasell?
Give ower mann! git
the spelk oot yor an
e eye afore yi taak
aboot the beam in y
a marra's. Divint fo
rgit: ye've ti give
aall ya money away f
or ti git ti heaven
Me, aa cannit wait t
o inherit the orth.

where's it aall ganna end?
(1967)

ee, alan byekar, ye
luk leik butta would
n't melt in ya mooth
.ye're a bonny bairn
but ya nowt but trou
ble. Aa'll be hevin
words wi' ya mam. Ye
'll niva come to owt
D'ye even belang roo
nd heor? Hadaway or
aall caall the poli
s. Where's it aall g
anna end? Nase alwi
z in a bluddy buik!

Dispatches

Dispatches

Just a heads up
if your walking
your dog down
towards blaydon....
My mam and
her friend
were walking
my dog
and my mams
friends dog
a few days ago.
My dog
was off
the leash
as he was
running
in a field
where he
couldn't escape....
My mam turned
around and
this man
appeared
out of no where,
on a phone
tried to steal

the dog...
I've invested
in a baseball
bat which
I can legally
carry
as long as
its not
in a threatening
way....
However
should said
Mr Dog Snatcher
try to get my dog
his face
will meet
my new friend
Bob...
Bob the face
basher.
Keep your eyes
peeled everyone.

(Jaime Scully Curry)

could anybody blame people
for not having faith
in the police in our area
they are more interested
in running around
in unmarked cars
nicking people
for traffic offences
making money out of hard
working people
camera Van's making money
if you live on a council estate
like a lot of us your
at the bottom of the ladder
for help with crime

(Neil Foster)

Please get them shops
down and blocked off
for those ppl
in Wesley Court
my mam lives
in one of the bungalows
and I don't like the fact
nothing has been done
about the gangs
hanging around the shops
its disgusting the way
this council has let them
shops go Ive lived on the estate
all my life we were like
one big family
them shops were great
I watched them being built
we all had respect
for ppl not like these
little shits who
are running wild
around the estate
yous need to protect
all the residents
in Wesley Court

(Maureen Nicholson)

I was on the bus
from the town
on Saturday
and as we got
to the park
kids started
to throw things
at the bus
it was very bad
and made me jump
driver stopped
further up
to see
if every body
was okay said
the week before
that there was
a girl with a pram
and the window
got shattered
and bits of glass
went into the baby's pram
touch wood they were
not hurt what the hell
is wrong with
these kids doing that
they must use
the buses and there family's

(Linda Eliot)

Fr Donnelly was a bit of a firebrand!
When I lived in Cleadon Close I used
to cut across the Churchyard there
to get picked up for Work at the
Westway Garage. He stopped me one day
and told me I was Trespassing and stop it.
I said the Lords Prayer says Forgive those
that Trespass against you. Ffs I thought
he was going to explode and never seen
that colour Purple on anyone's face since.
BTW I walked the long way round after that.

(Paddy Cairns)

Joe Bowman and Bob Morris

Joe Bowman

When aa was a bairn, Aa'd gan to the glassworks
to bring him his bait,

Aa'd watch him work, blae the bubbles
o' hot glass.

When he had nee job, nee money for drink,
he'd help wi' the hoosework, scrub the floors.

When he worked, we'd never knaa
what payday would bring.

Me ma would watch the clock; when it struck six,
"That's it! He's not coming hyem."

We didn't knaa when we'd see him again,
the morra, or for a canny few days,

till he'd spent aall his pay
on beer an' pitch-n-toss.

What would we eat?
A body cannit live on fresh air.

When the women in wor courtyard
hord what happened, they'd send thor bairns roond;

they'd knock on the door wi' a few coins:
"me Ma says to give this to Mrs Bowman".

Aa divint blame me Da, he had a hard life;
he had sixteen brothers and sisters

a faather who beat his mother,
started drinkin as a bairn,

an when he was oot o' work, nee money
for drink, he was a lovely fella.

Bob Morris Speaks

the 1926 strike
for the miners
was nae such bloody thing
it was a lock-oot!
every miner
everybody employed
at the pit
or aboot ti be
got fowteen days notice
an it torned oot
thi wad employ yi again
if ye tuk a fowty percent
reduction
that was the strike
how much was Aa gettin?
Aa'll explain
it as well as Aa can lad
for ten year
Aa was hewin coal
for one an tuppence-
h'apenny a ton
an on top o that
there was a slidin scale
wi had up ti a hunerd
an twenny per cent

mind ye even
a hunerd an twenny percent
on top one an tuppence
happeny doesn't bring
ye much for a ton o coal!
fowty percent was
a big reduction for us -
coppers, aye, whey ya jes
working for coppers
so it was a big reduction
wey wi refused
an we wor on strike
we come up to May
whey Aa say strike –
we wor locked oot -
from middle o May
an we didn't start
work agen til the
December we wor oot aall
that summer what
a lovely summer it was!
the only way yi
could git relief
in them days was to gan
to what yi caall
The Guardians an
the Guardians was hard
buggers there was offices

set up in different places
where me, wor lass
and wa one bairn went
they give iz a voucher
for twelve shilling
in cash an that hadda
keep yi see but when
the strike was ower
wi had to pay it
aall back it was
kept oot wa pay
two shilling a week
we'd cadge some bones
off the butcher
different farmers might
give wi a few tornips
or a few tetties
an wi used to form
soup kitchens
different locals
in the village would
mek soup
yi went wi yor can
and gorra can o soup
we wor well hard up!
but that died oot
and wi had ti
live the best way wi can
there was nee money

for busses if yi
wanted to gan to
Newcassell or Whitley Bay
or North Shields
yi just waalked
and thowt nowt aboorit
however when wi got
back to pit Aa think
it was the back end
o November we worn't
back a month
withoot any ado
aboot it they gev wi
another fowty percent
reduction that's
eyty percent
wi couldn't dee
nowt aboorit - we wor
beat yi see well
and truly beat -
they was bloody
hard days after that
an that went on
till the second war
cause the thorties
they was bludy bad days
by god they was
hard days

Aa hewed coal an
the best men couldn't
get nee more than
thorty five bob a week
that had ti keep
yor hoose and family
aye thorty five bob a week
it was cruelty mann!
an the gaffer spoke
ti yi as if yi
was just muck
yi don't answer him back o no

Notes:

Twittersonnet is a form invented by Robert Sheppard. It has 280 characters (like a tweet) split over the 14 lines of a sonnet, giving 20 characters per line, including punctuation. All of these pieces are based – some very closely – on real conversations.

There are recordings of me reading some of the Twittersonnets on the online magazine Molly Bloom:
https://mollybloom21.weebly.com/alan-baker.html

I'd like to thank Molly Bloom editor Aidan Semmens for publishing these pieces.

Charlie Carr was my next door neighbour. He was a welder and shop steward at Swan Hunter's shipyard. The shipyards were nationalised in 1973, but didn't survive the Thatcher era.

"Dispatches" are taken from posts made in 2020 to a social media group for the housing estate in Newcastle on which I grew up. Personal names and place-names have been altered to protect privacy but otherwise the texts are unchanged.

"Bob Morris Speaks" is a transcript of one of the entries in the British Library's Survey of English Dialects. The speaker was born in 1898 and at the time of the survey (the 1950s) was a retired miner. The recording can be found at https://sounds.bl.uk/Accents-and-dialects/Survey-of-English-dialects/021M-C0908X0001XX-0400V1

"Joe Bowman" is based on the reminiscences of my mother, born Mary Bowman, Newcastle-upon-Tyne, 1923, about her father, a skilled worker in the glass industry on Tyneside.

I am grateful to Kelvin Corcoran and Cliff Yates for their comments on the manuscript. Thanks to you both.

Alan Baker